Relaxing coloring book for adults with the illustrations inspired by India.

Enjoy coloring various mandalas, patterns, birds, elephants and Indian women in traditional outfit.

Imagine that you are travelling in this country full of colors.

Take your favourite media to color, use additional sheet of paper between pages to avoid bleeding to the next page.

Happy coloring!

Copyright © 2021 by Katya Suresh

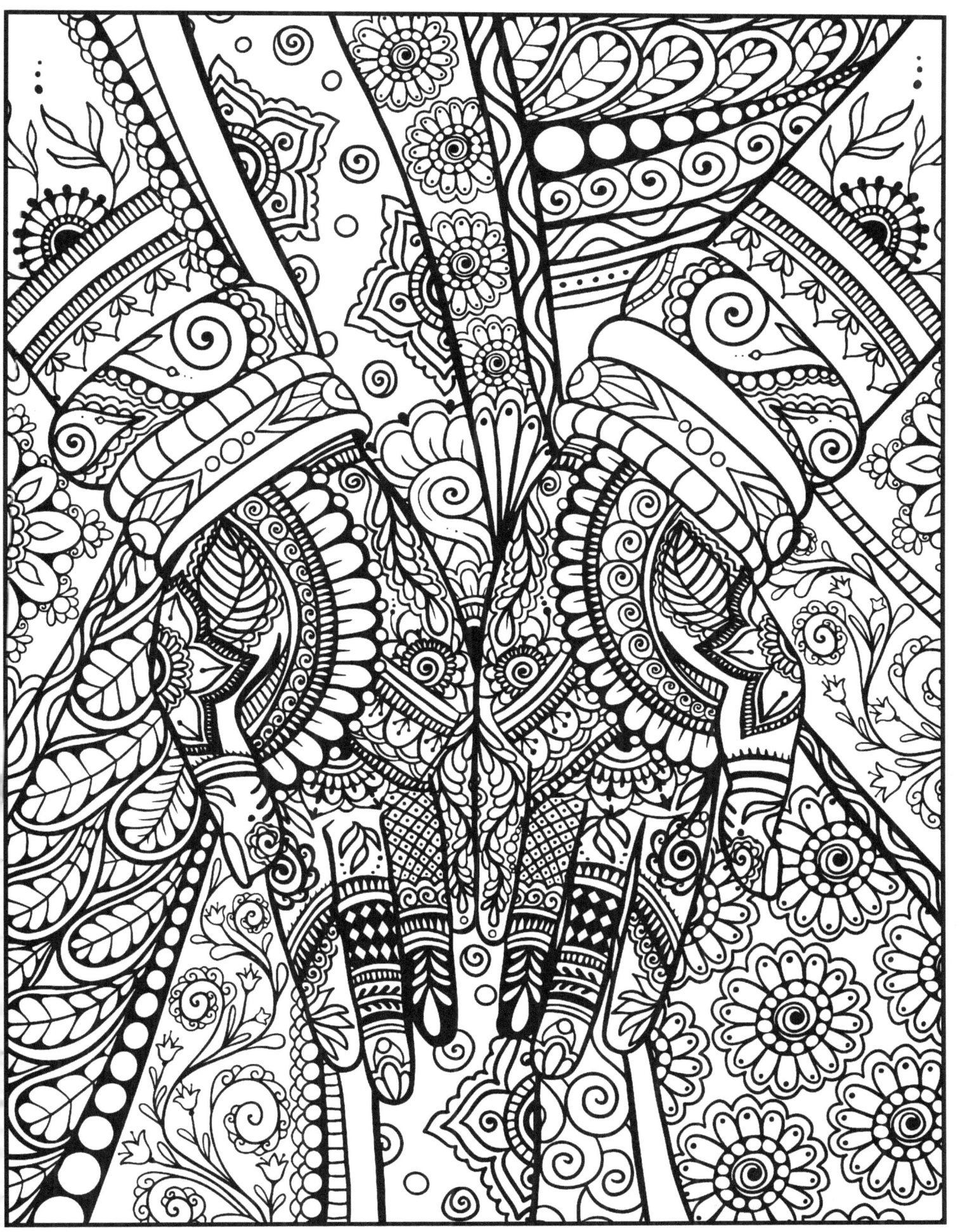

Copyright © 2021 by Katya Suresh

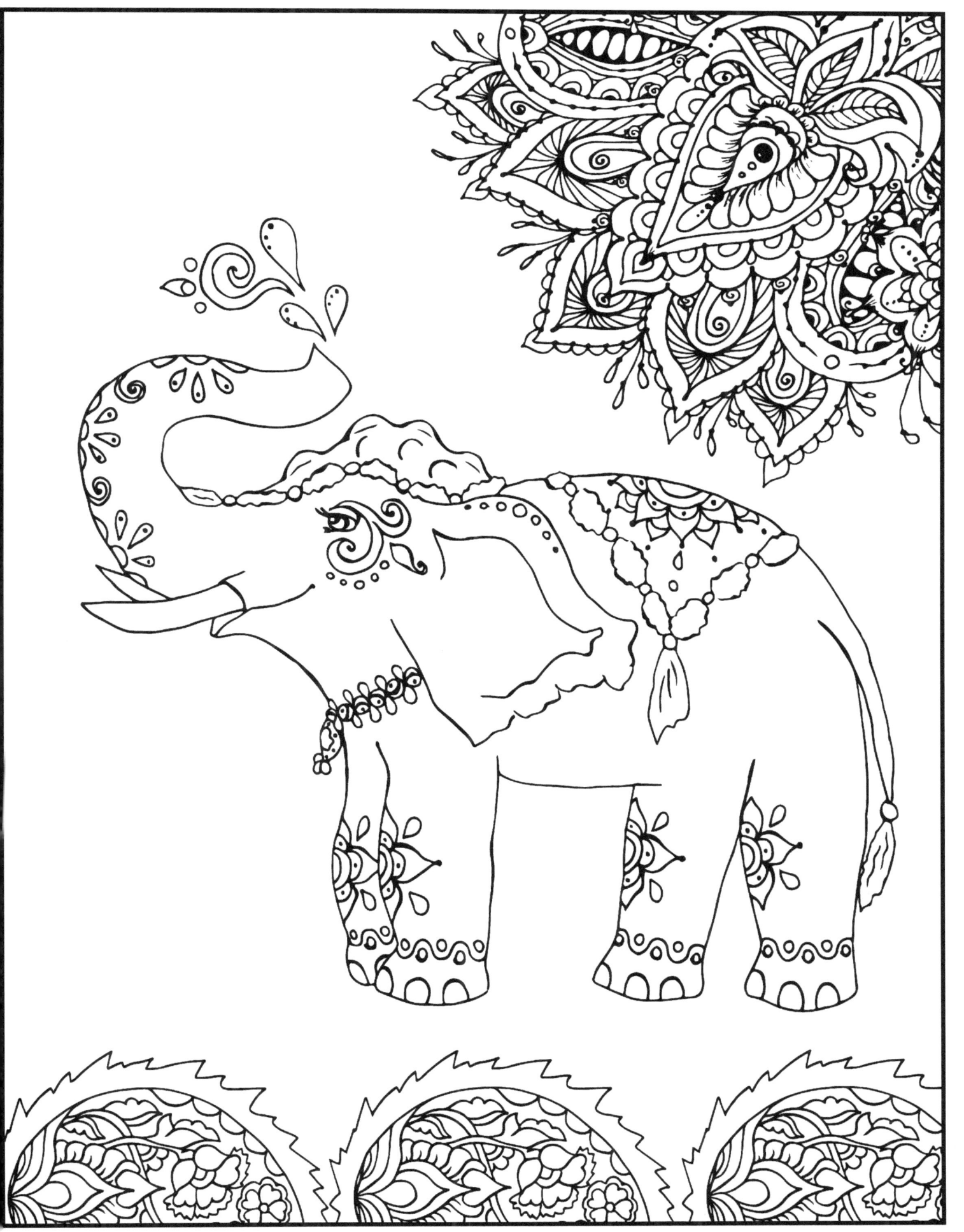

Copyright © 2021 by Katya Suresh

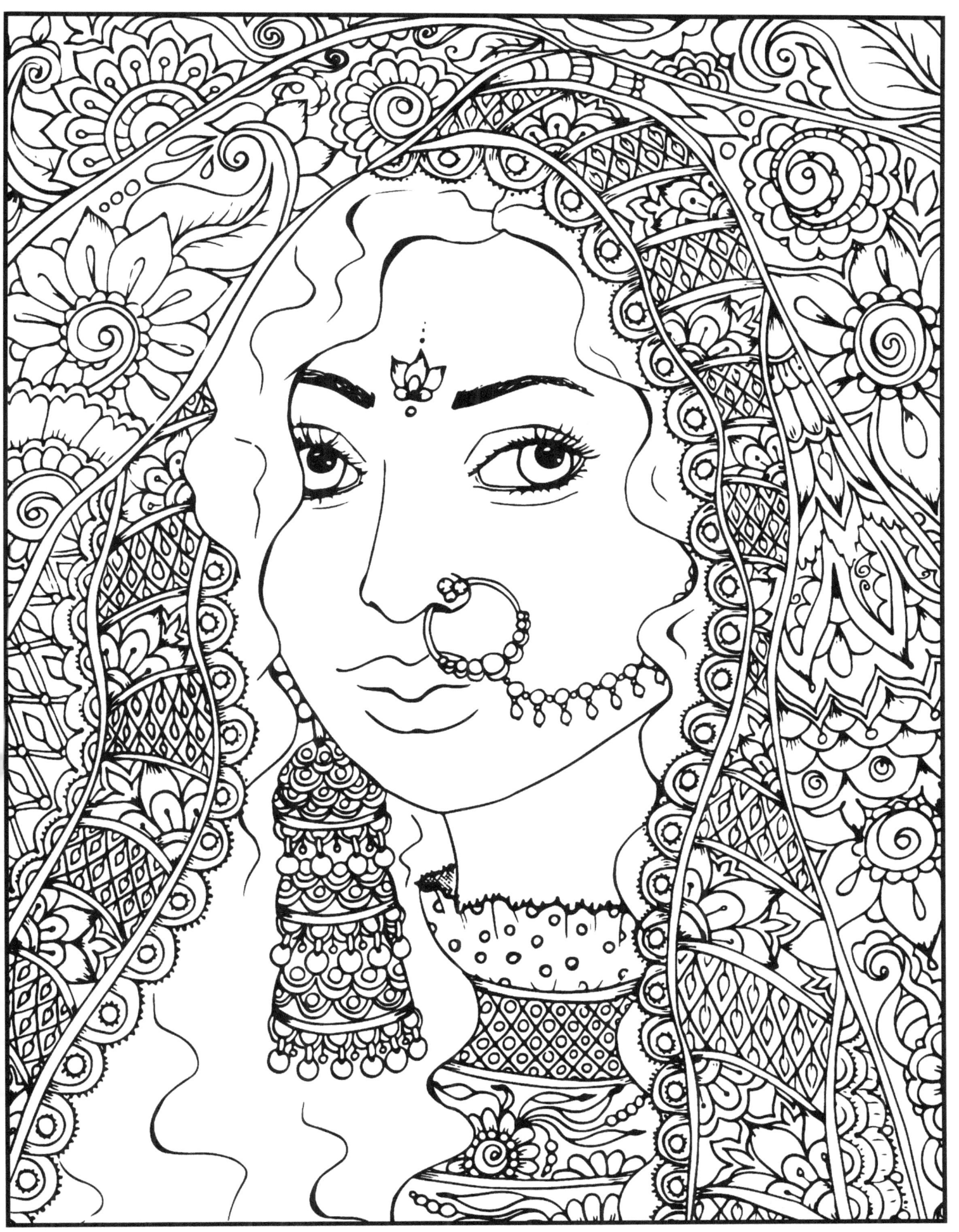

Copyright © 2021 by Katya Suresh

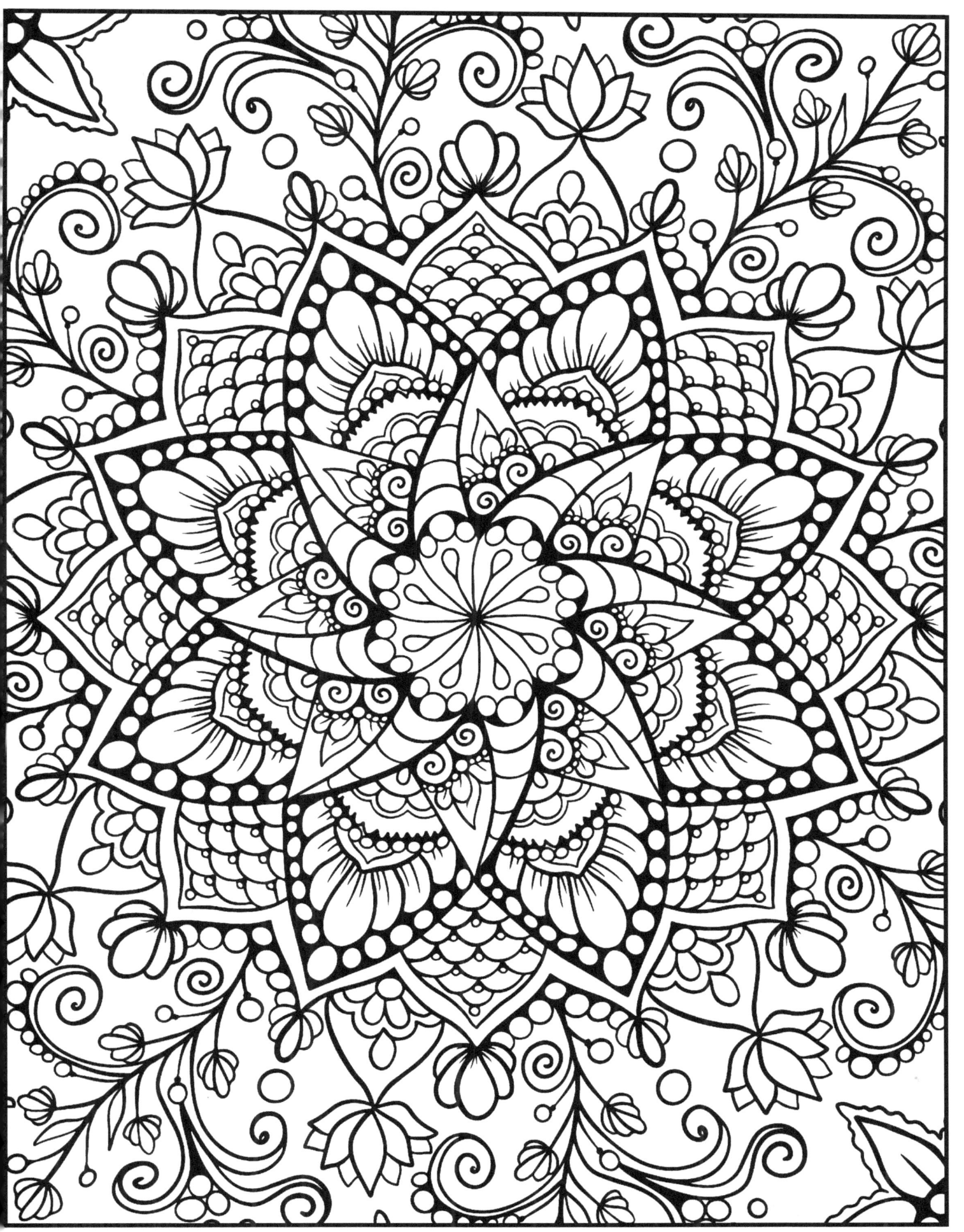

Copyright © 2021 by Katya Suresh

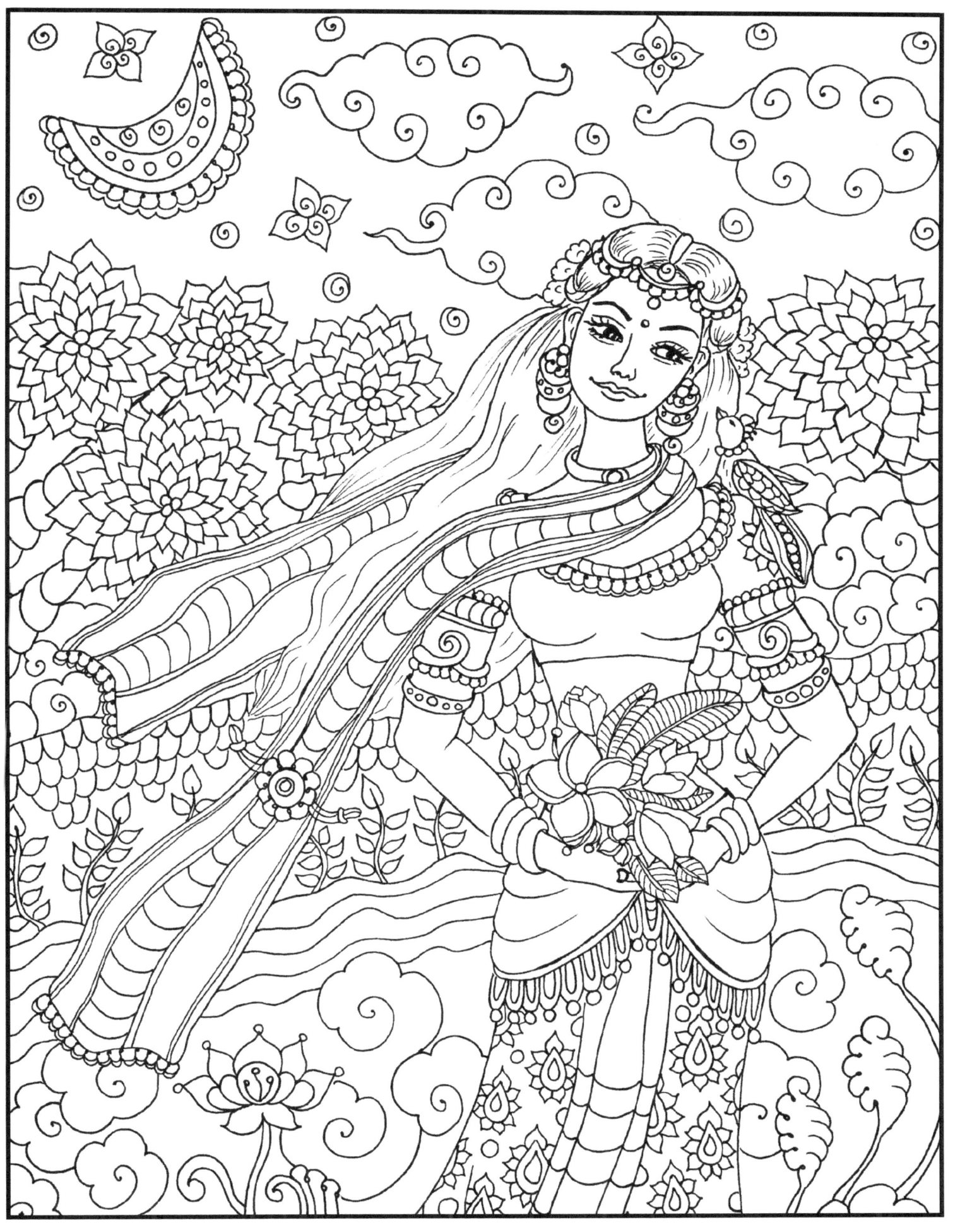

Copyright © 2021 by Katya Suresh

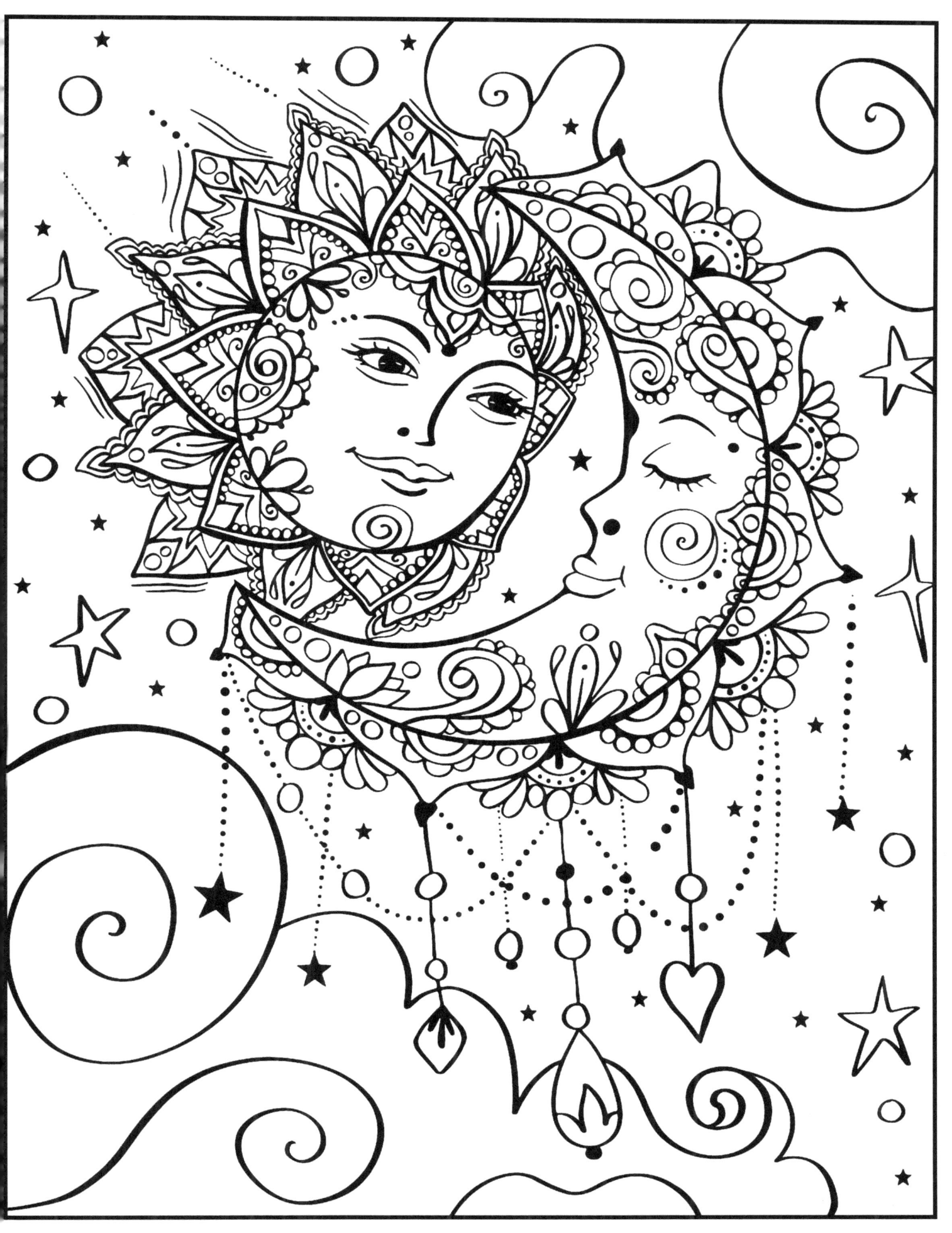

Copyright © 2021 by Katya Suresh

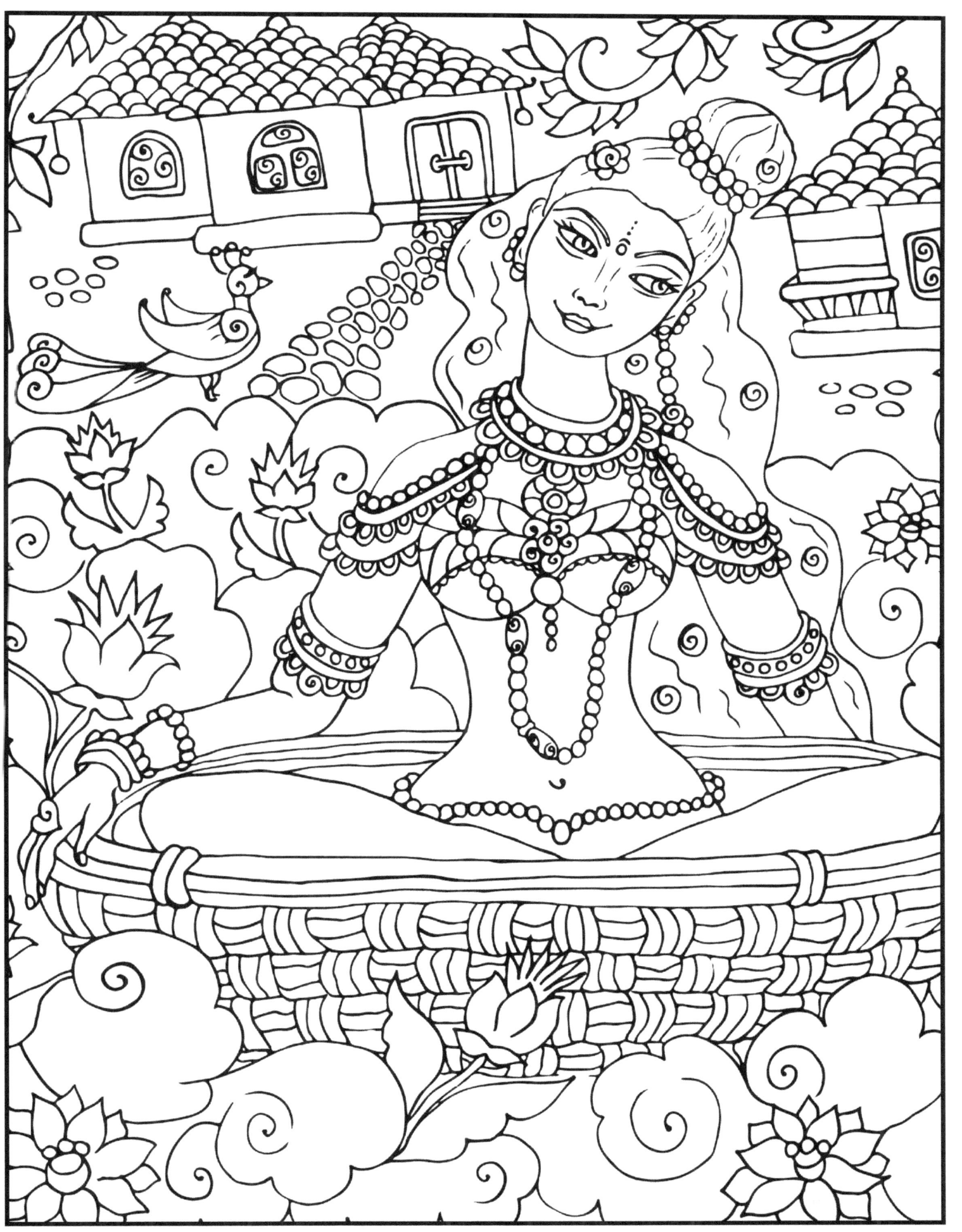

Copyright © 2021 by Katya Suresh

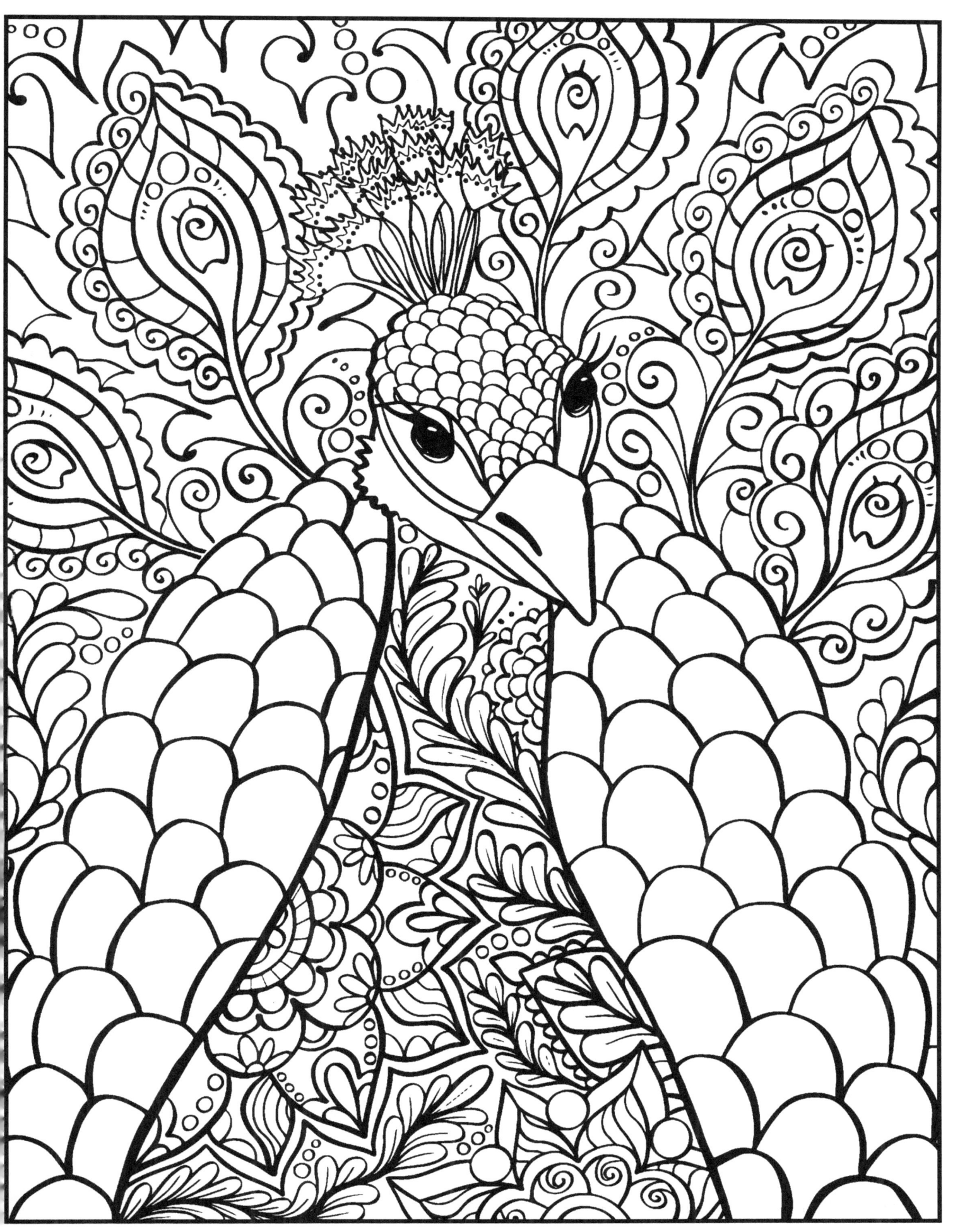

Copyright © 2021 by Katya Suresh

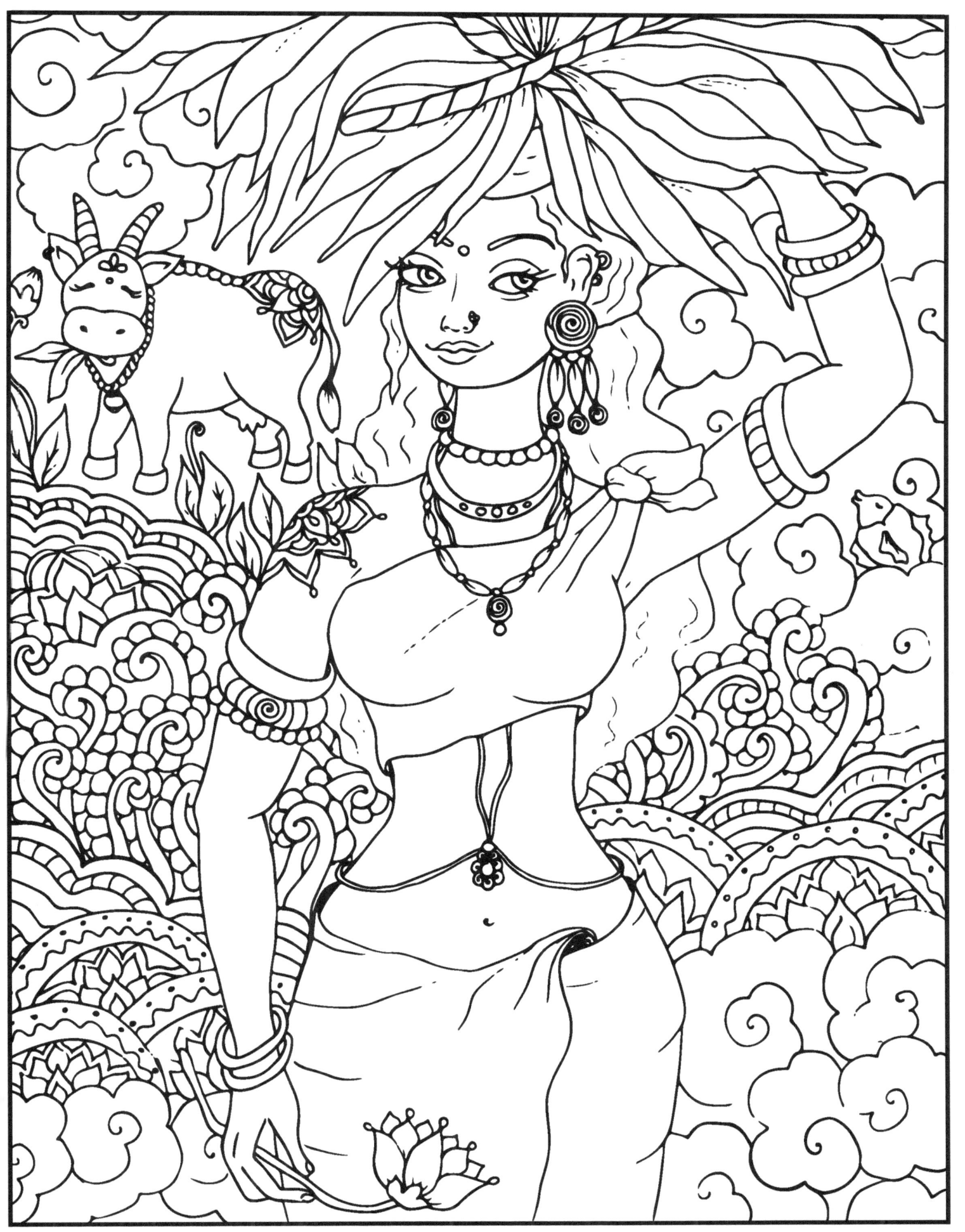

Copyright © 2021 by Katya Suresh

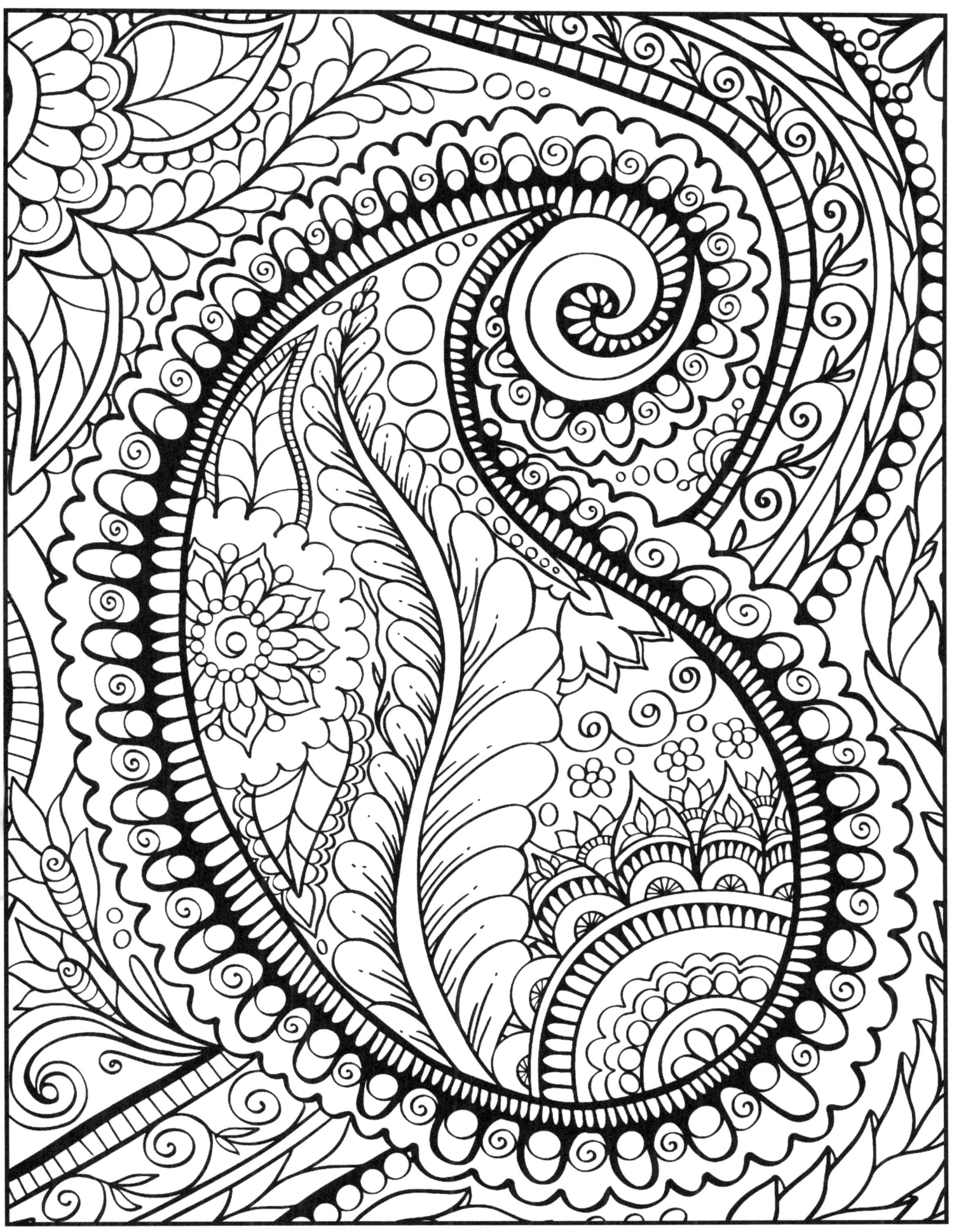

Copyright © 2021 by Katya Suresh

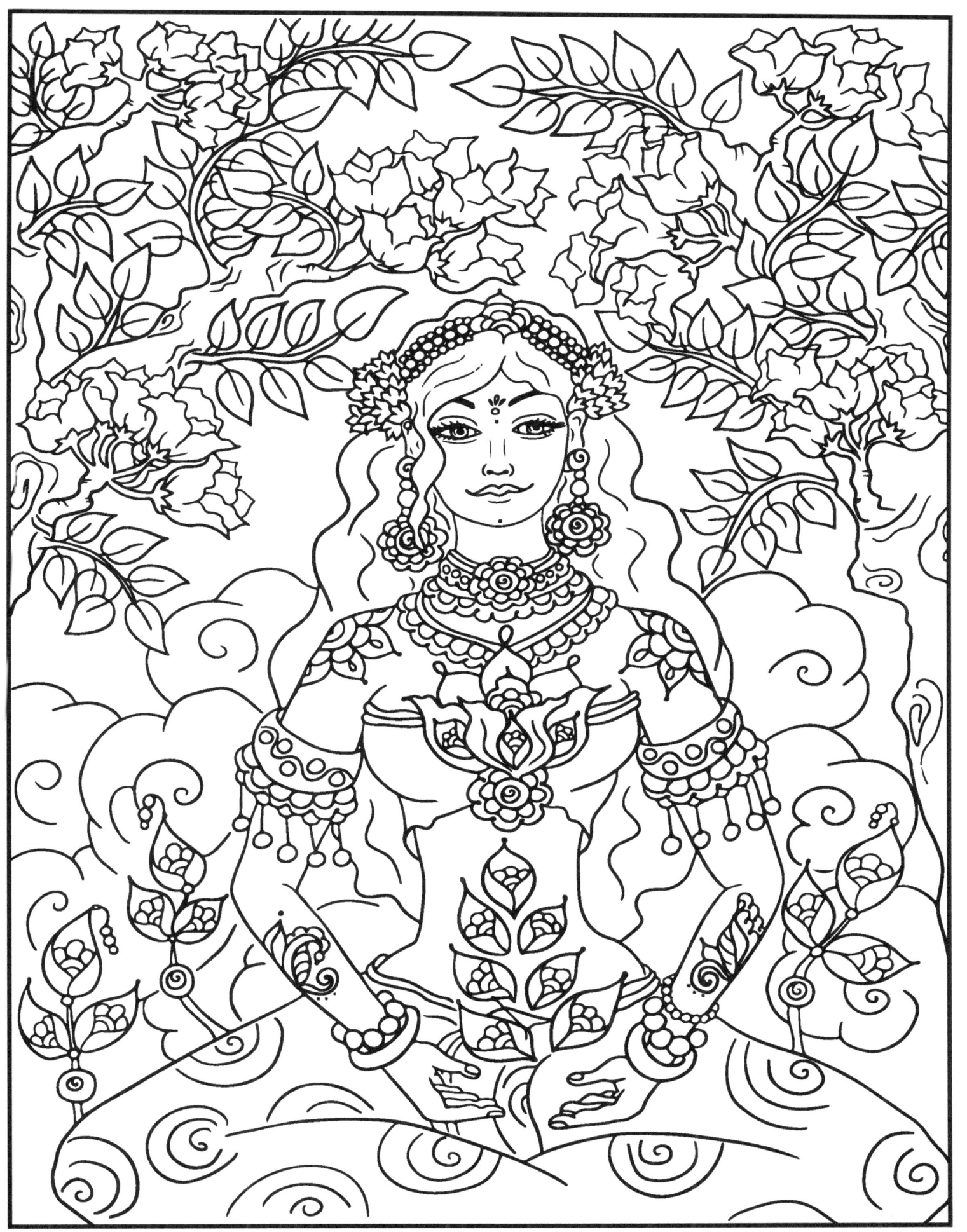

Copyright © 2021 by Katya Suresh

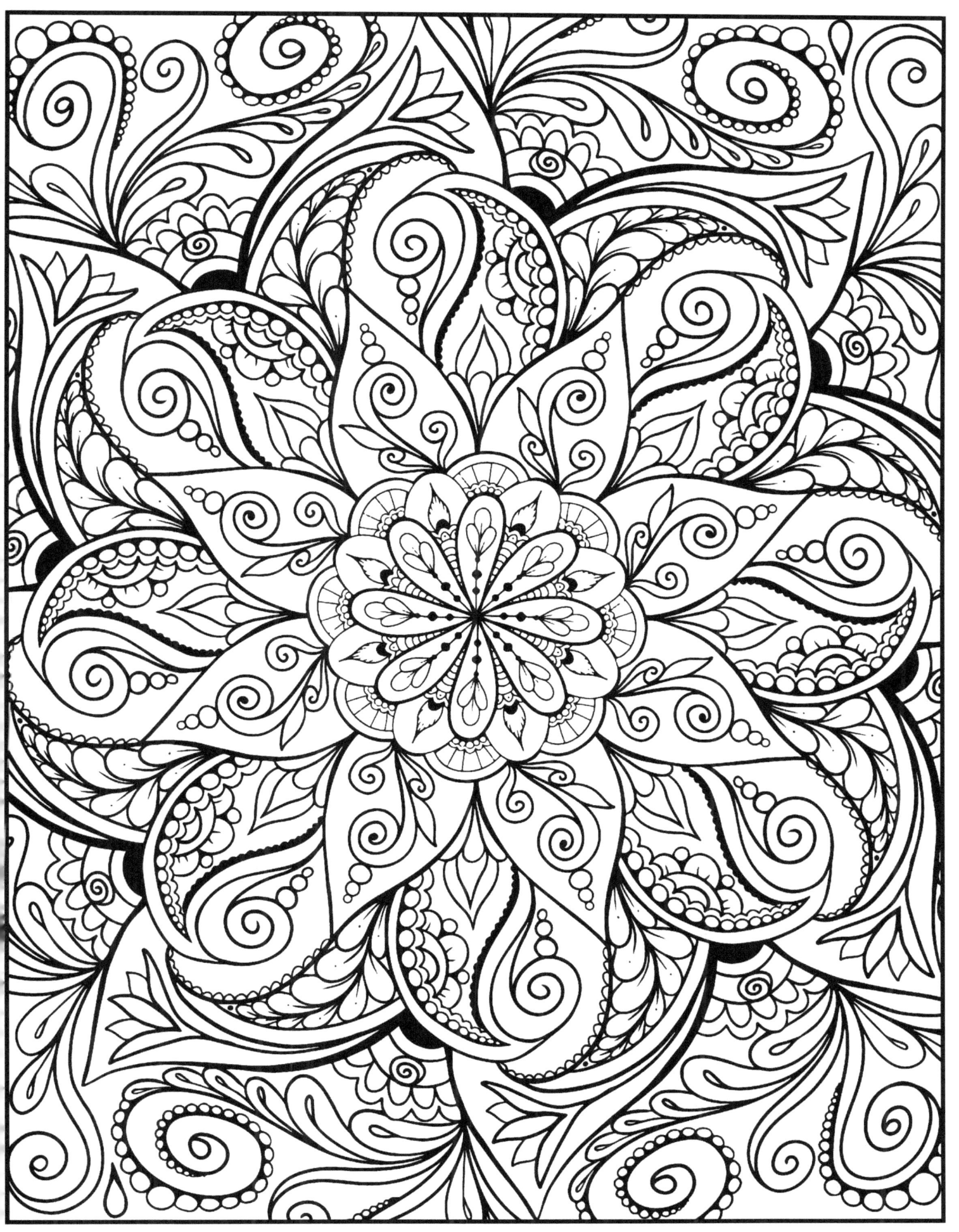

Copyright © 2021 by Katya Suresh

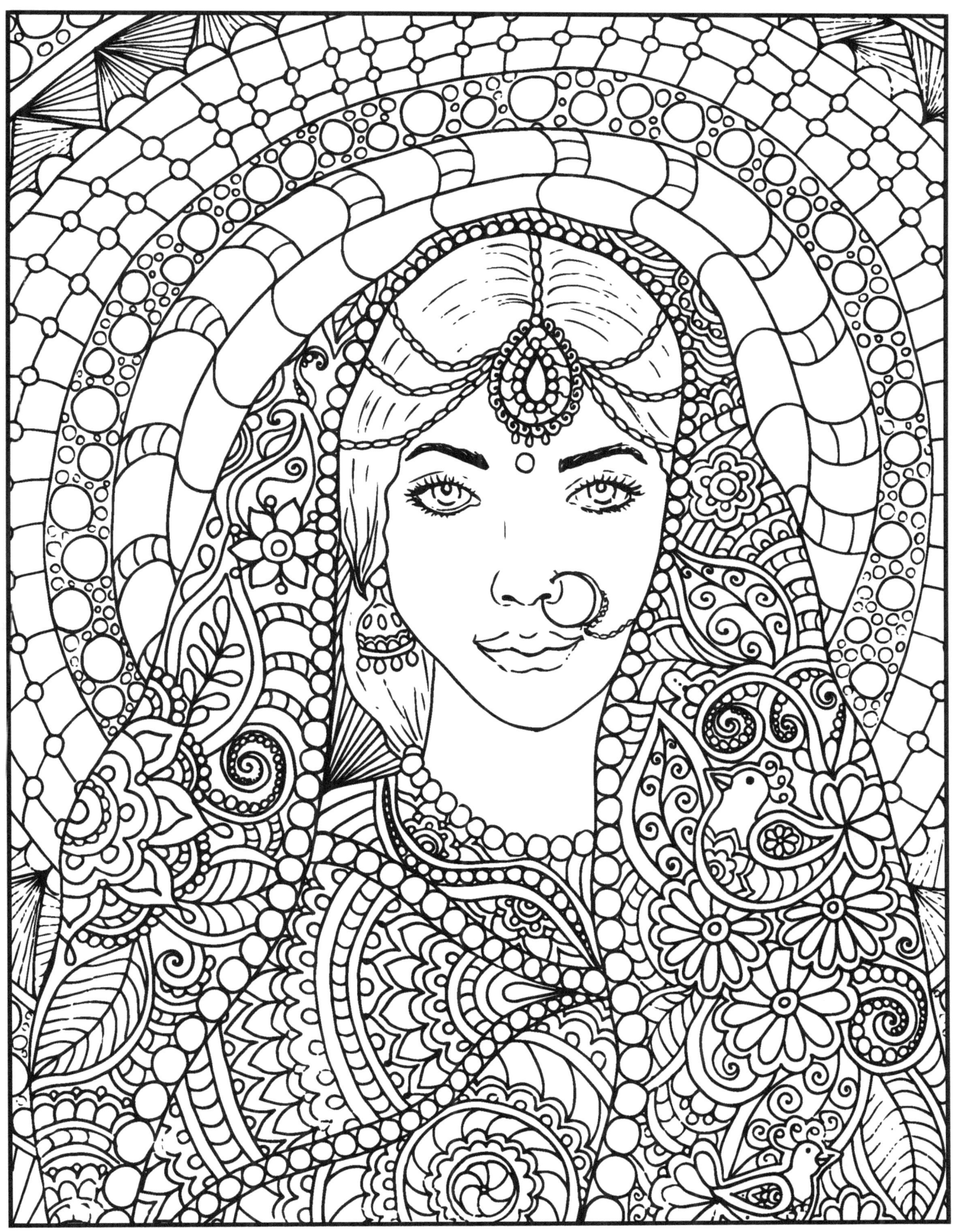

Copyright © 2021 by Katya Suresh

Copyright © 2021 by Katya Suresh

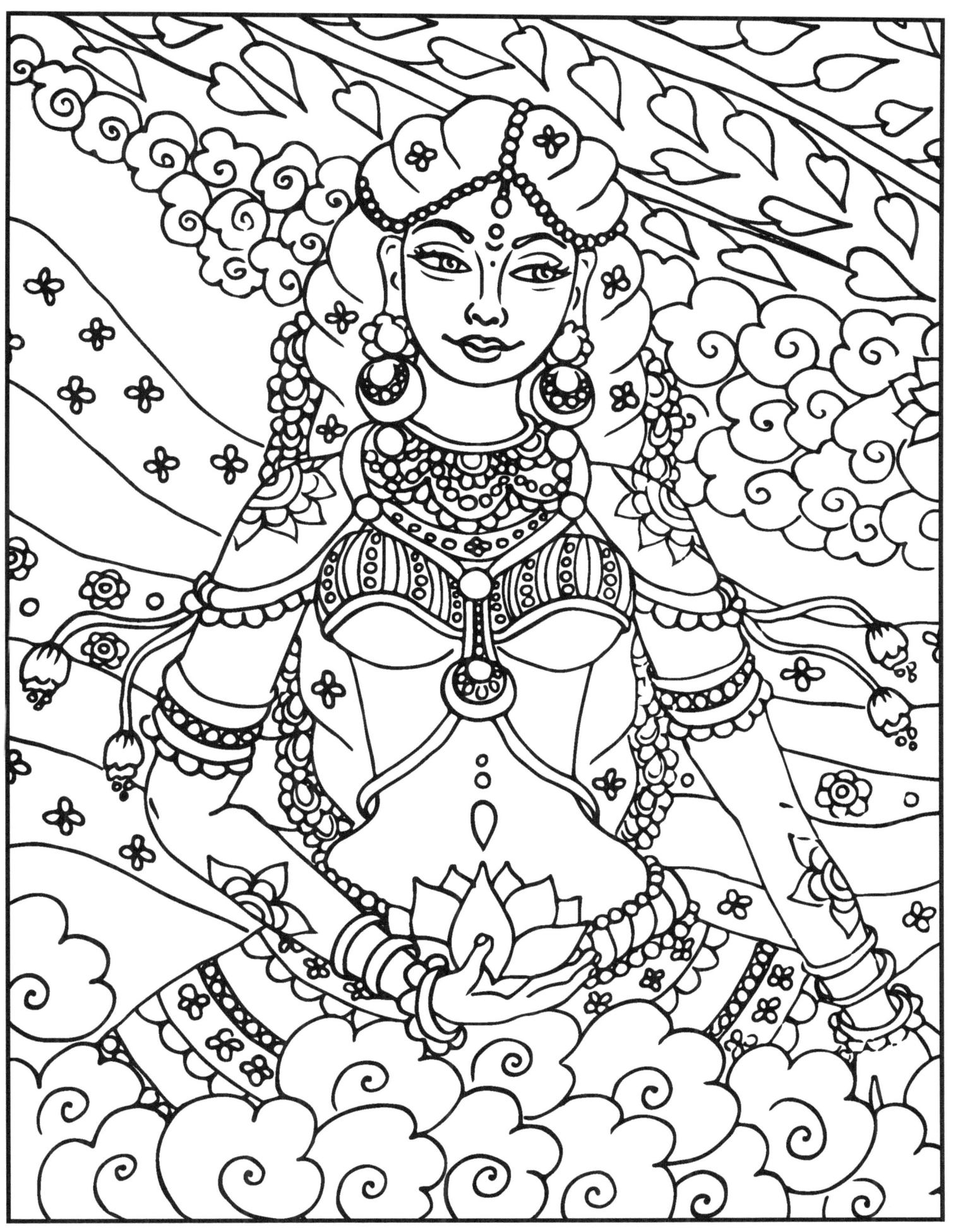

Copyright © 2021 by Katya Suresh

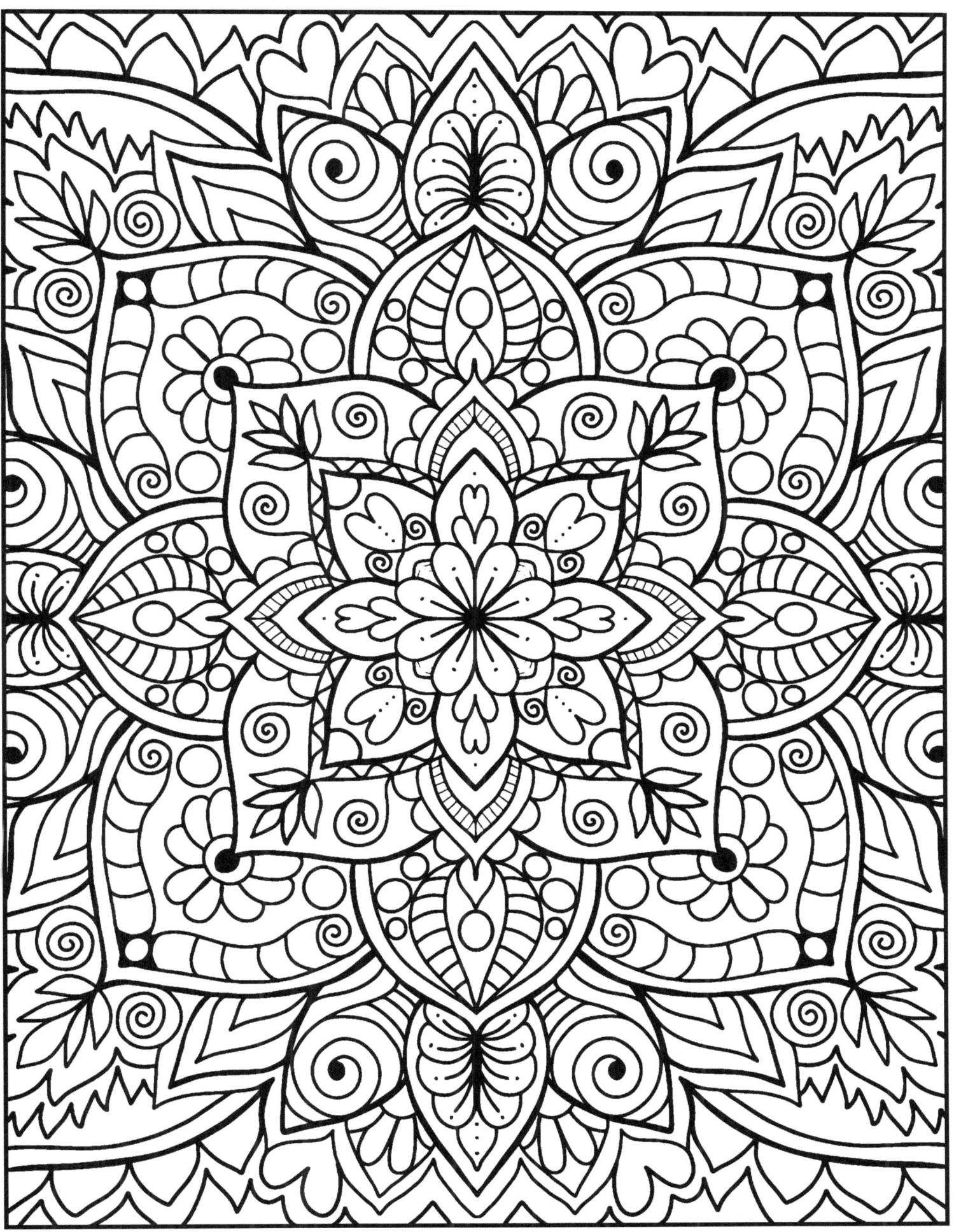

Copyright © 2021 by Katya Suresh

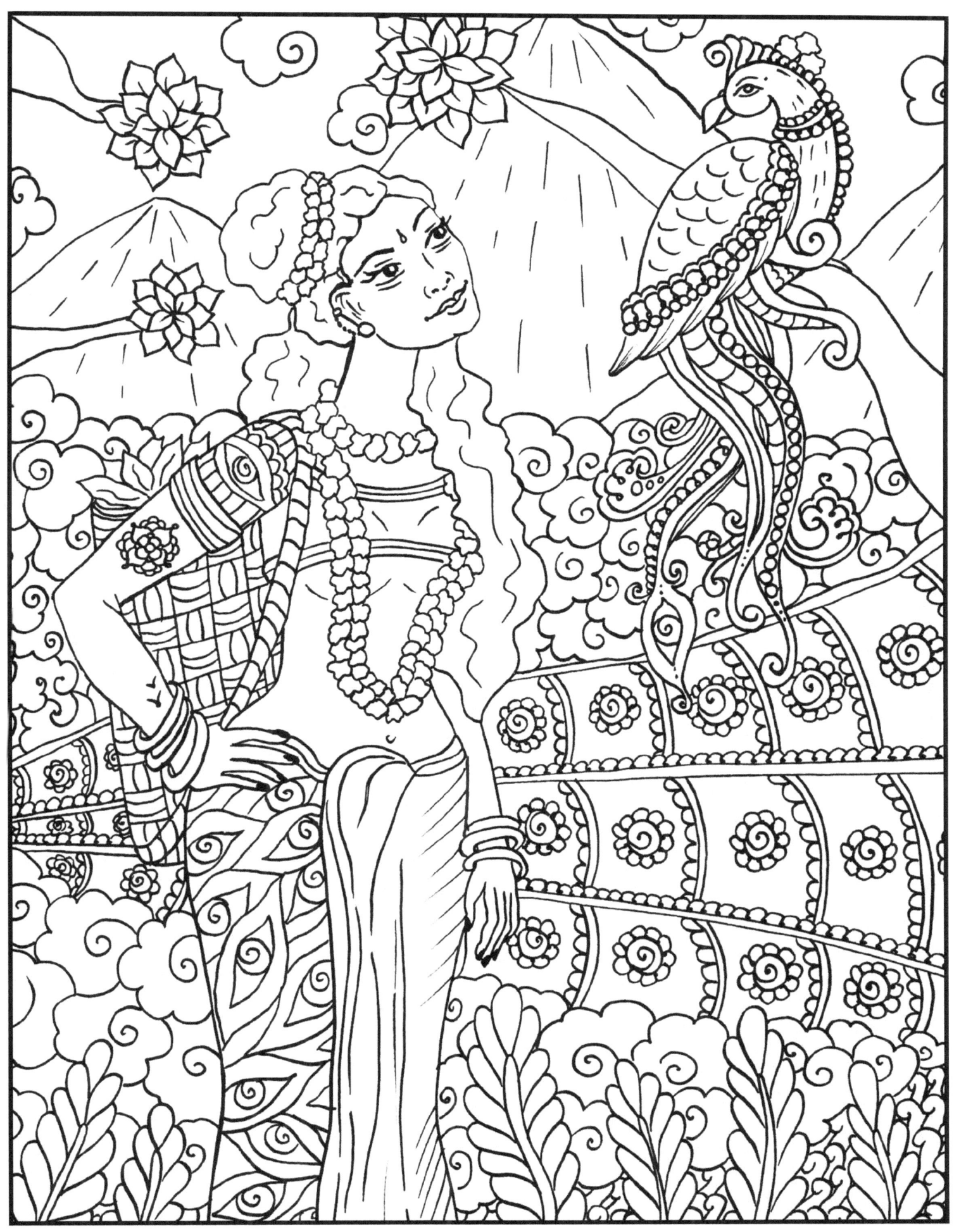

Copyright © 2021 by Katya Suresh

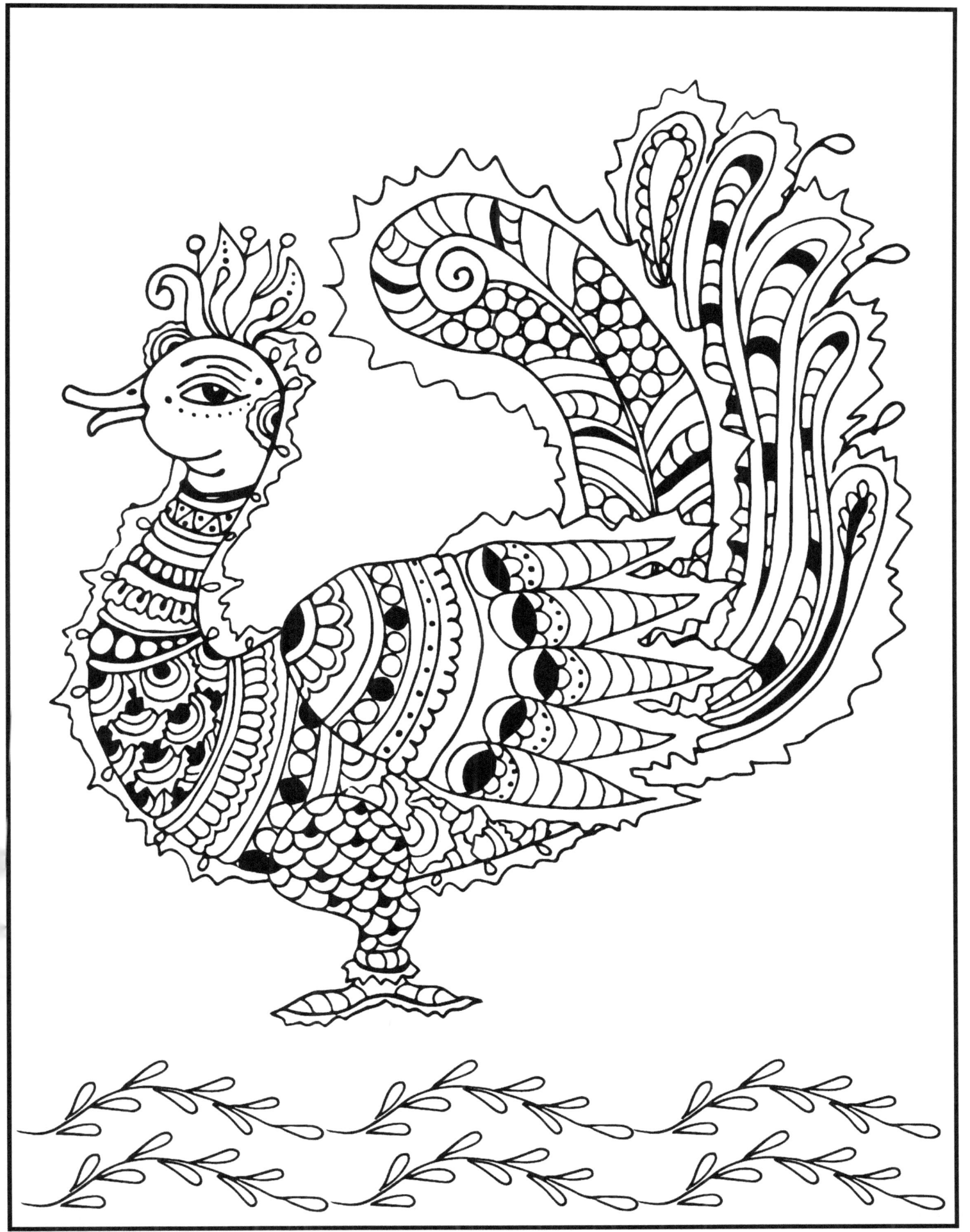

Copyright © 2021 by Katya Suresh

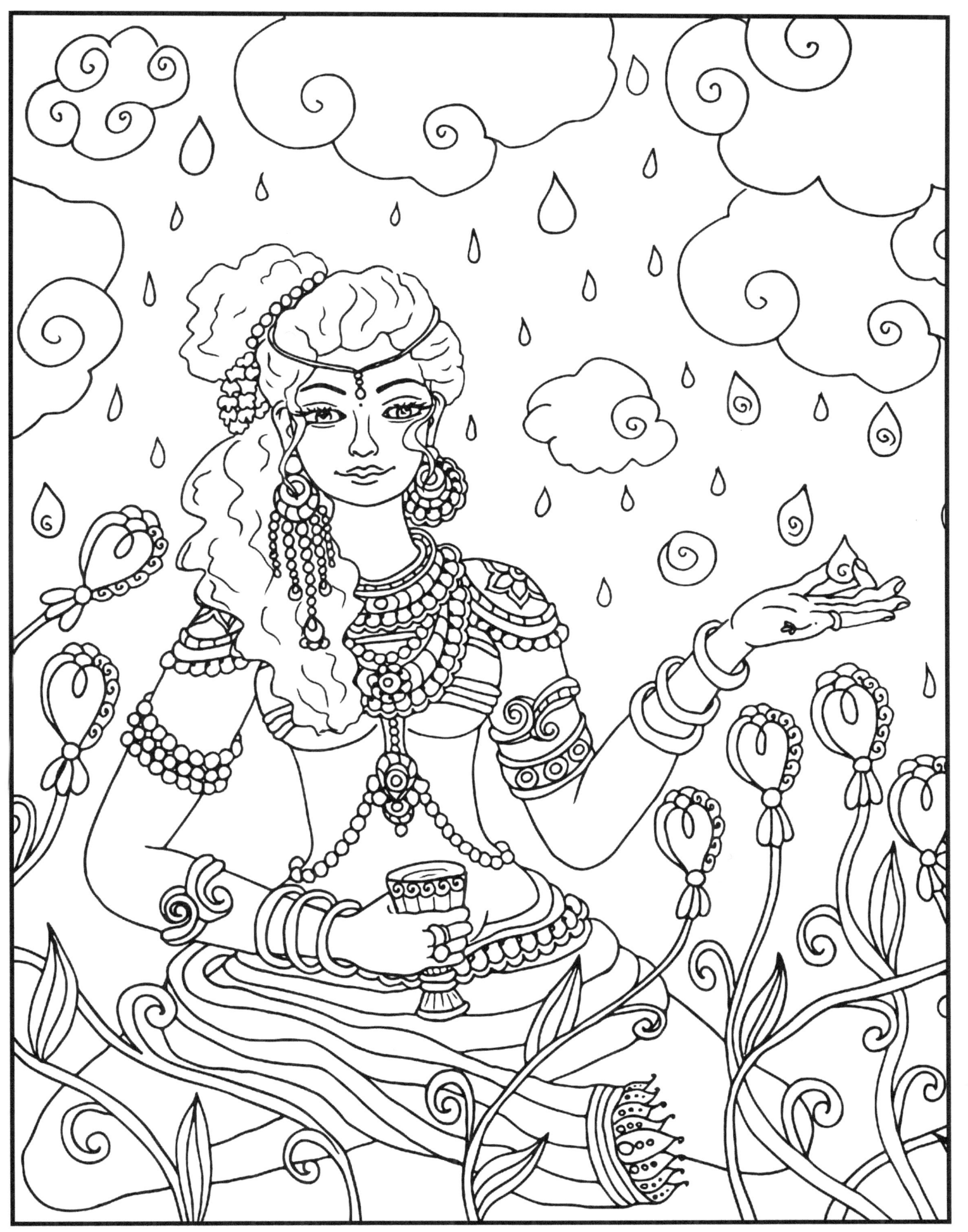

Copyright © 2021 by Katya Suresh

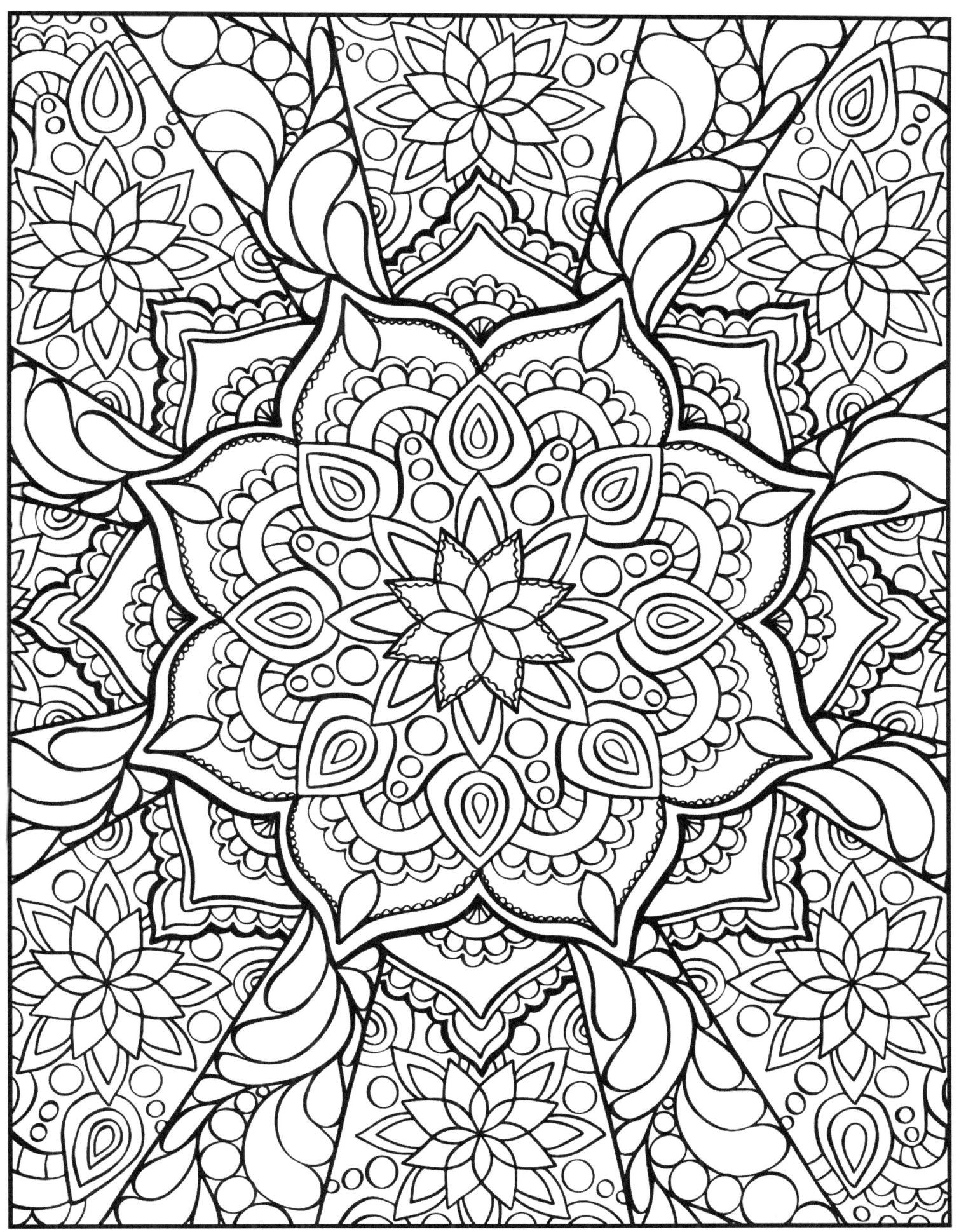

Copyright © 2021 by Katya Suresh

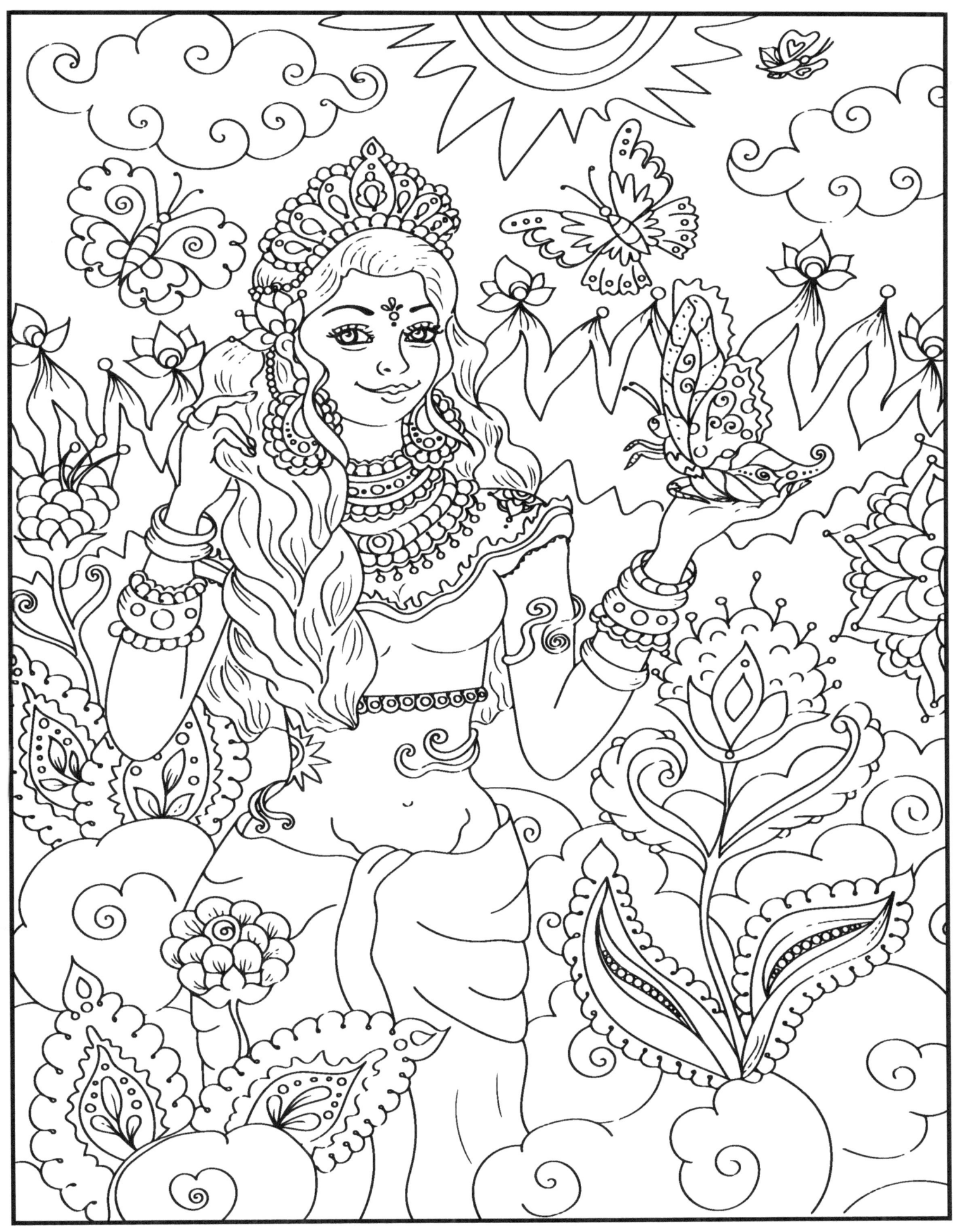

Copyright © 2021 by Katya Suresh

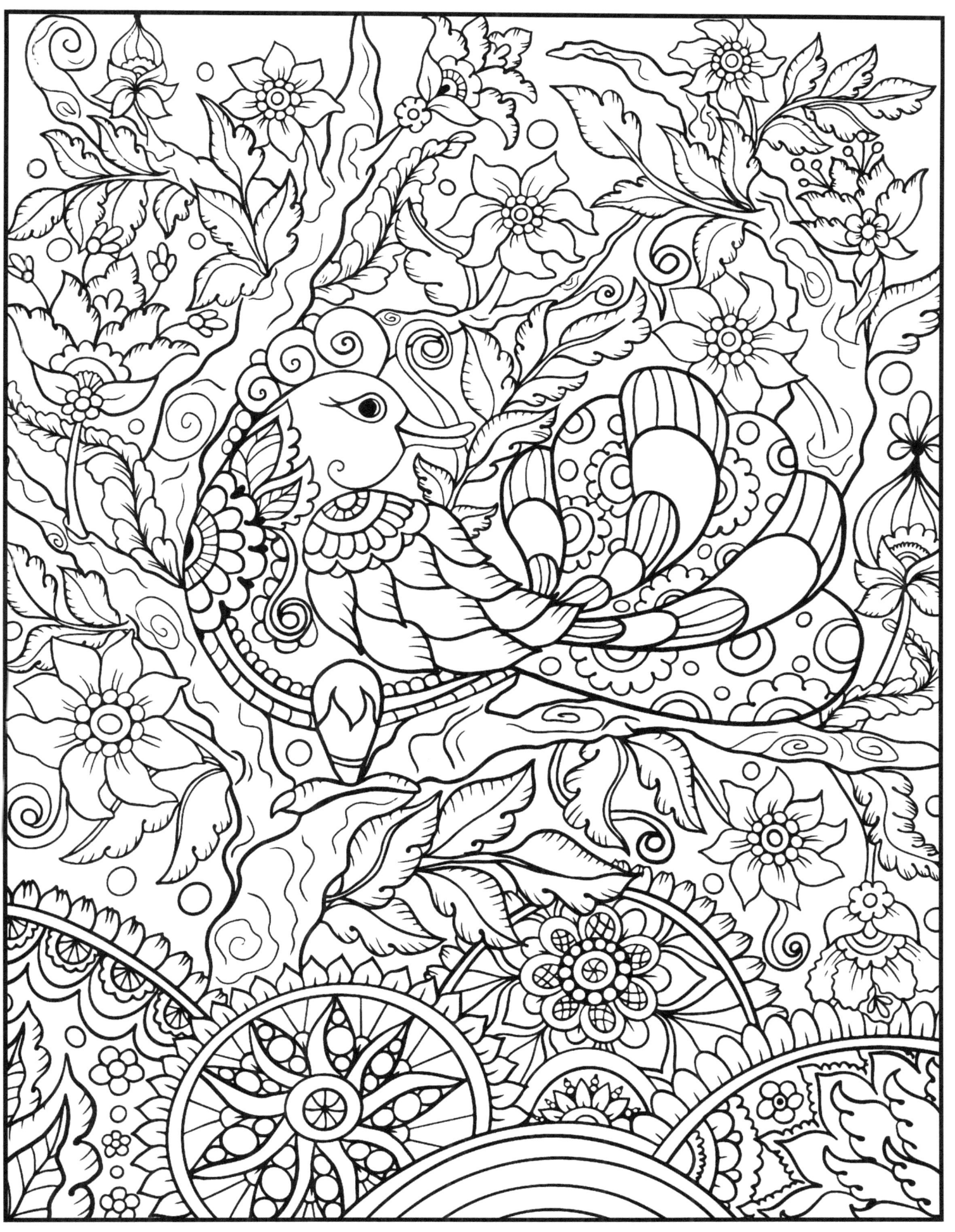

Copyright © 2021 by Katya Suresh

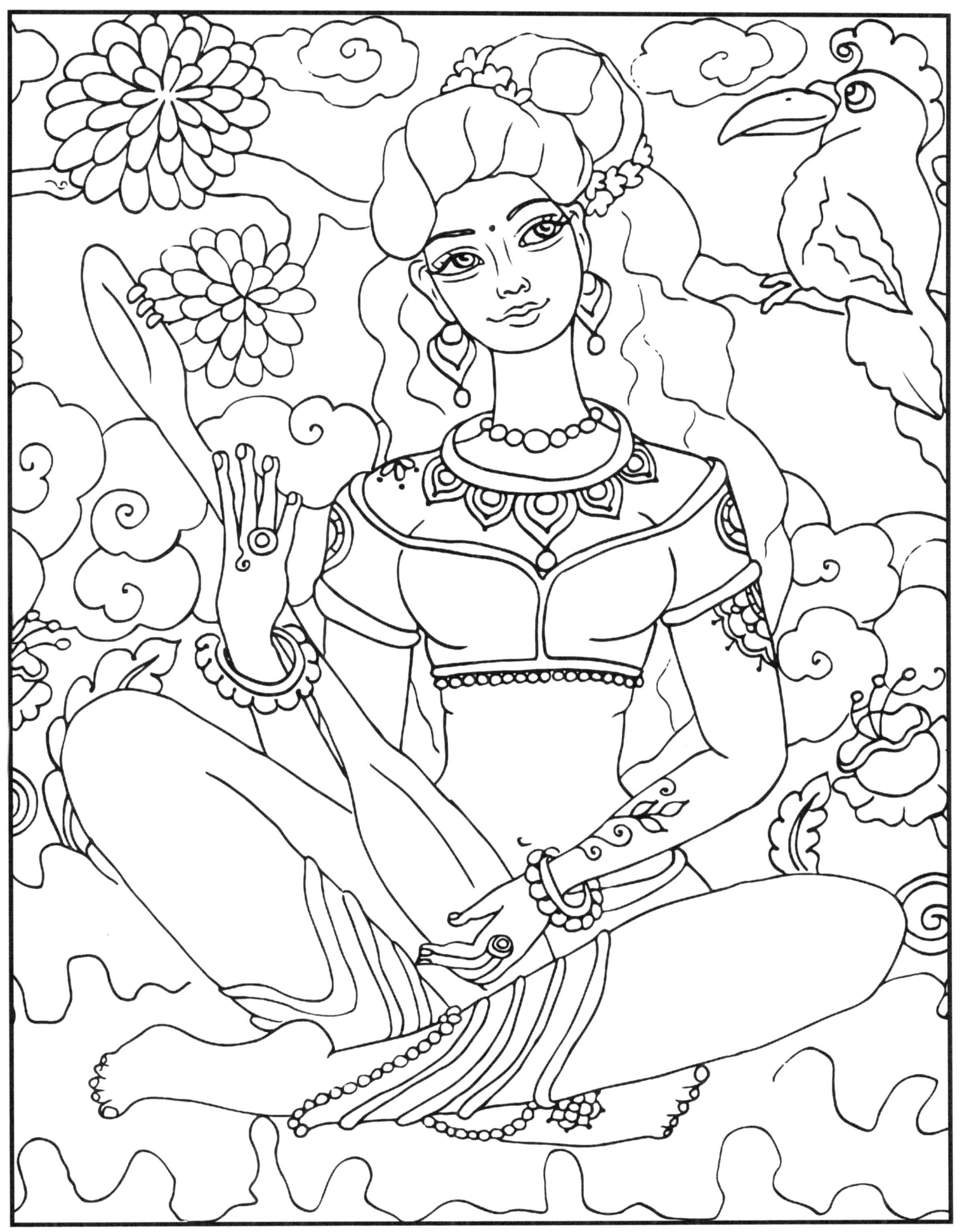

Copyright © 2021 by Katya Suresh

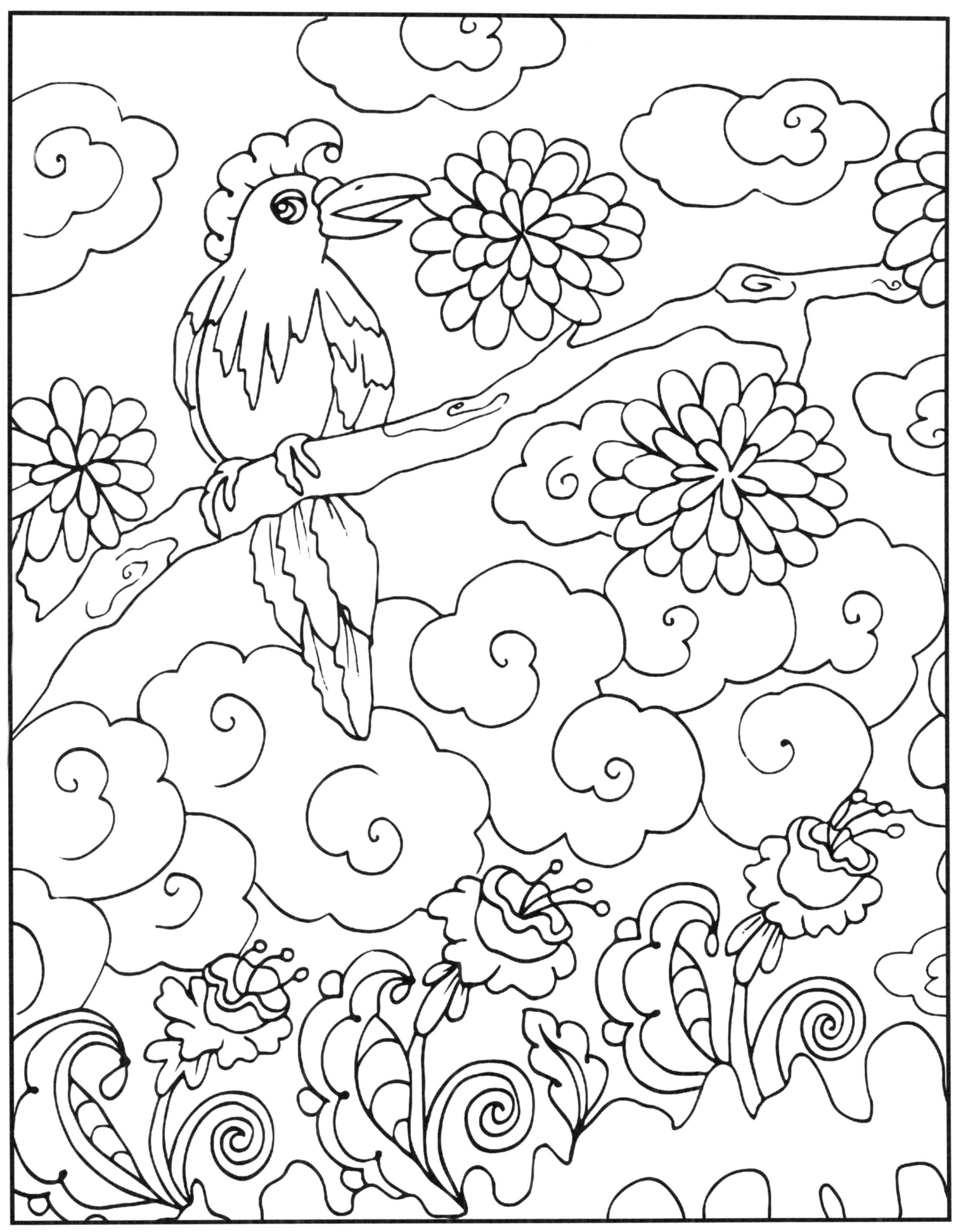

Copyright © 2021 by Katya Suresh

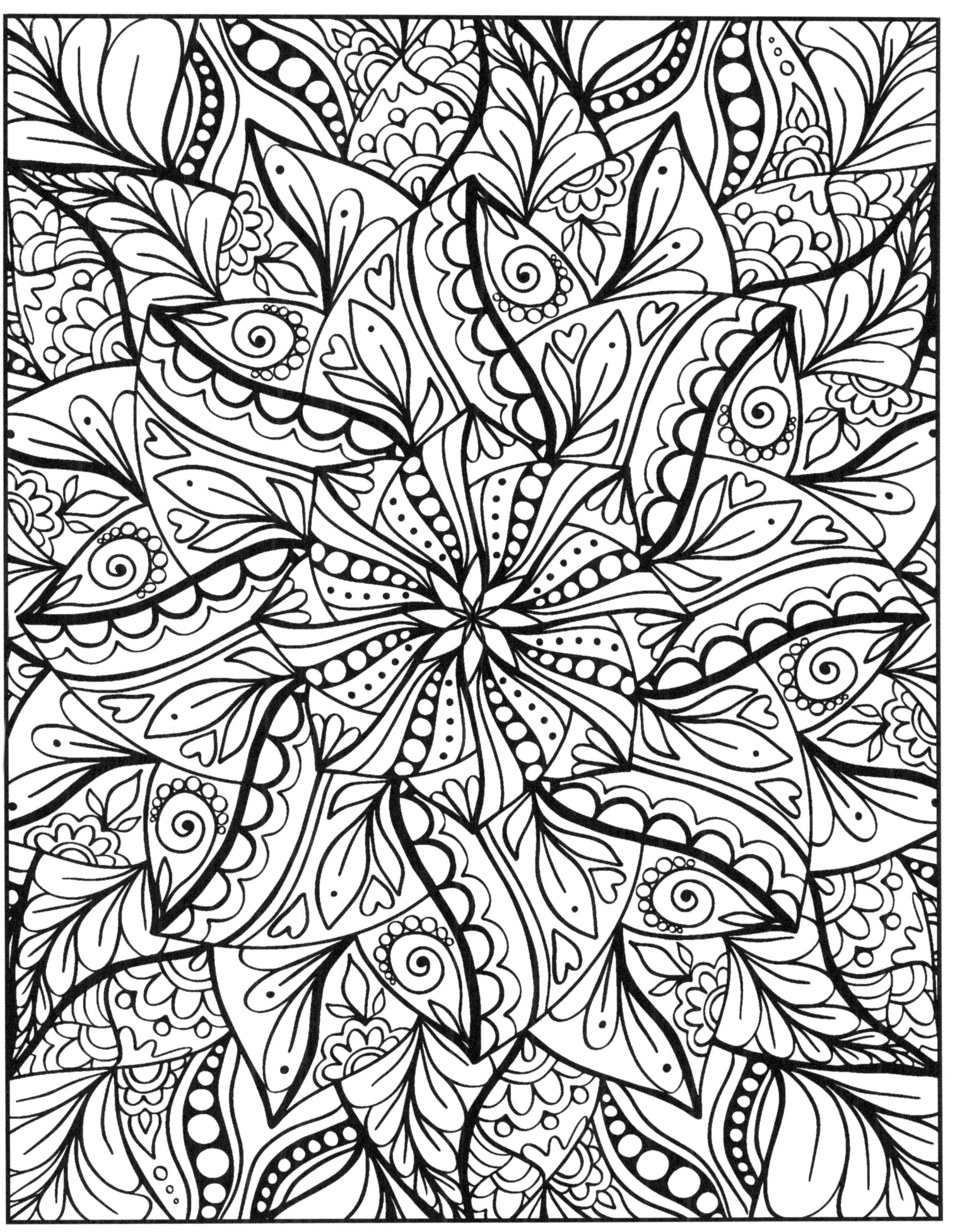

Copyright © 2021 by Katya Suresh

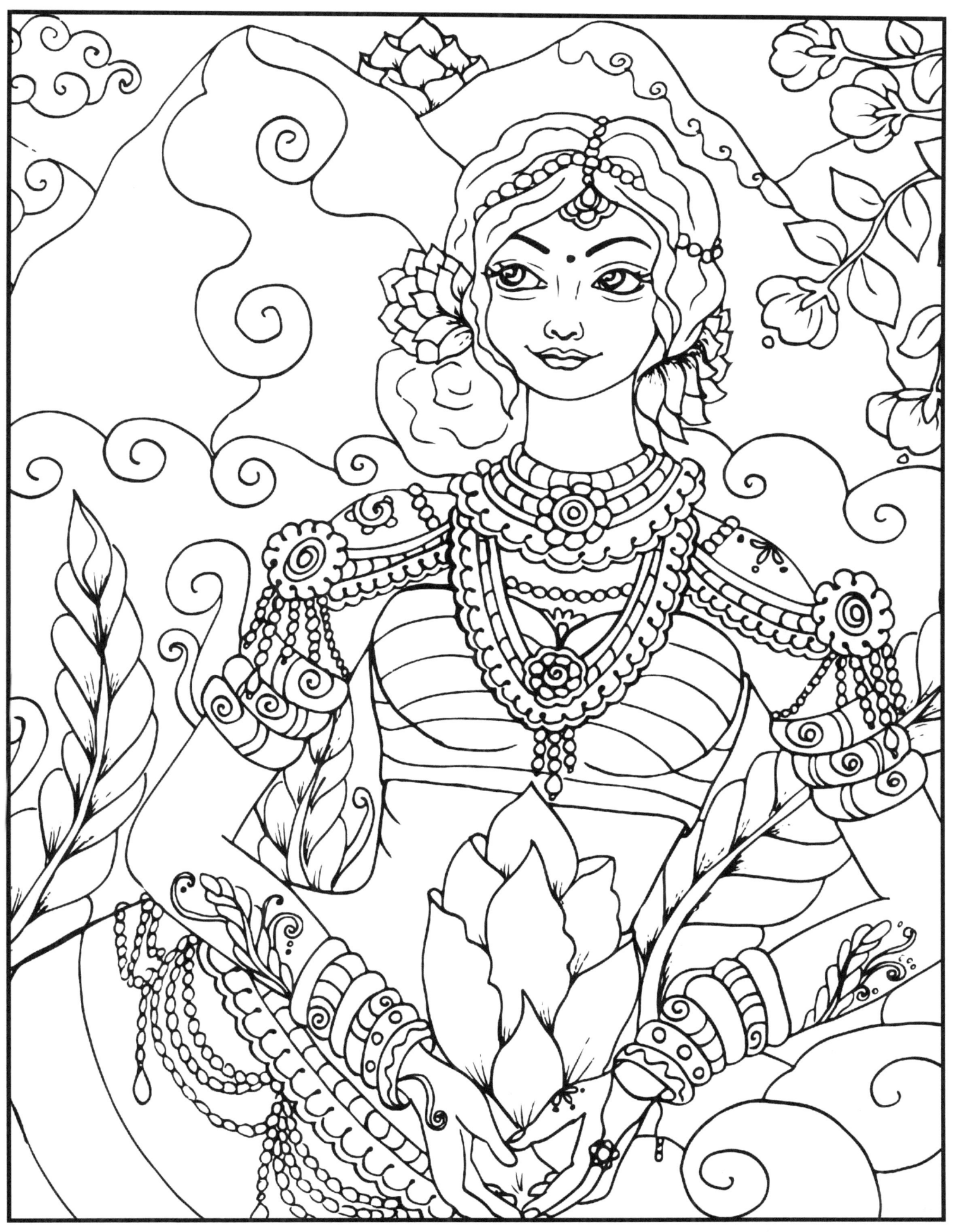

Copyright © 2021 by Katya Suresh

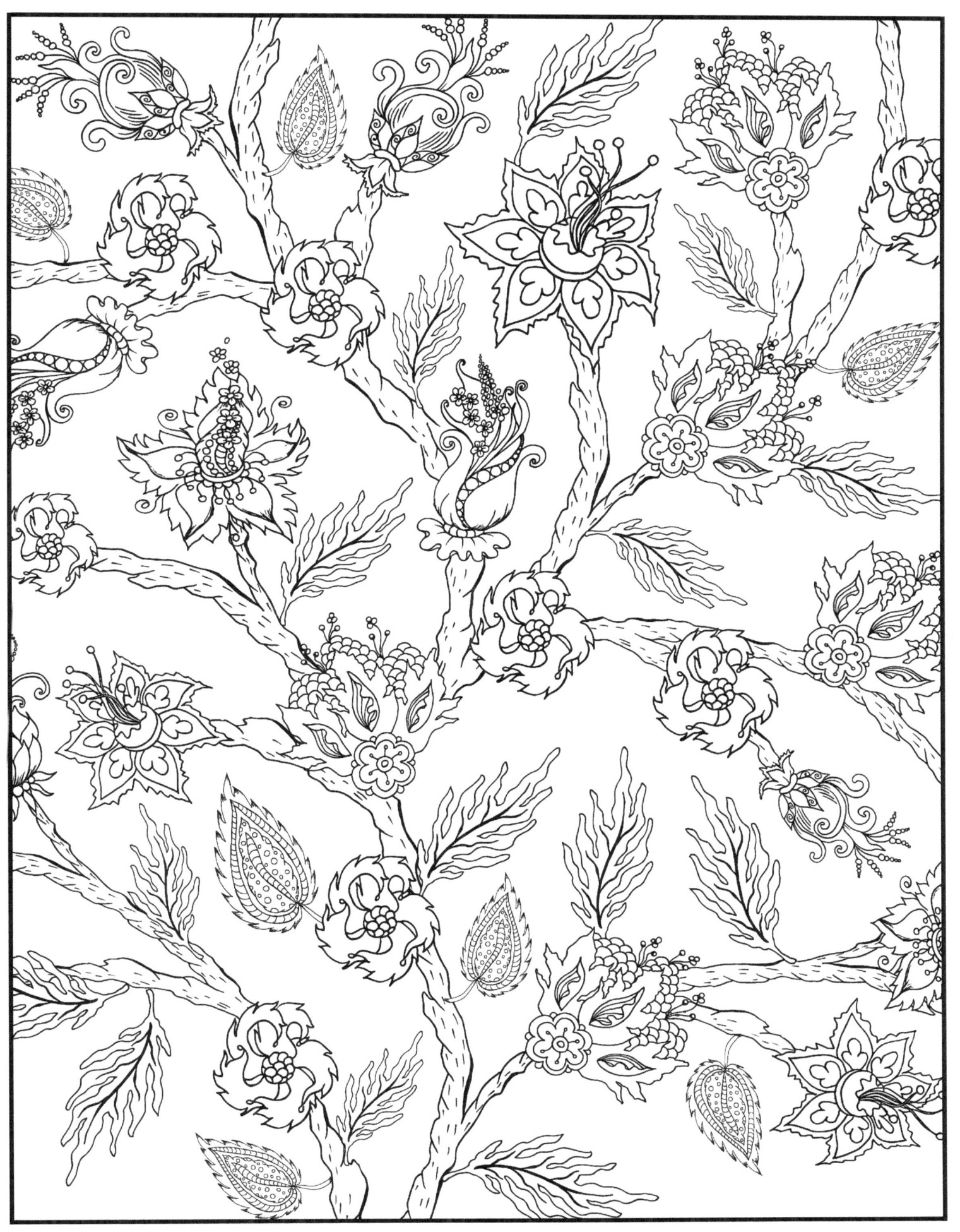

Copyright © 2021 by Katya Suresh

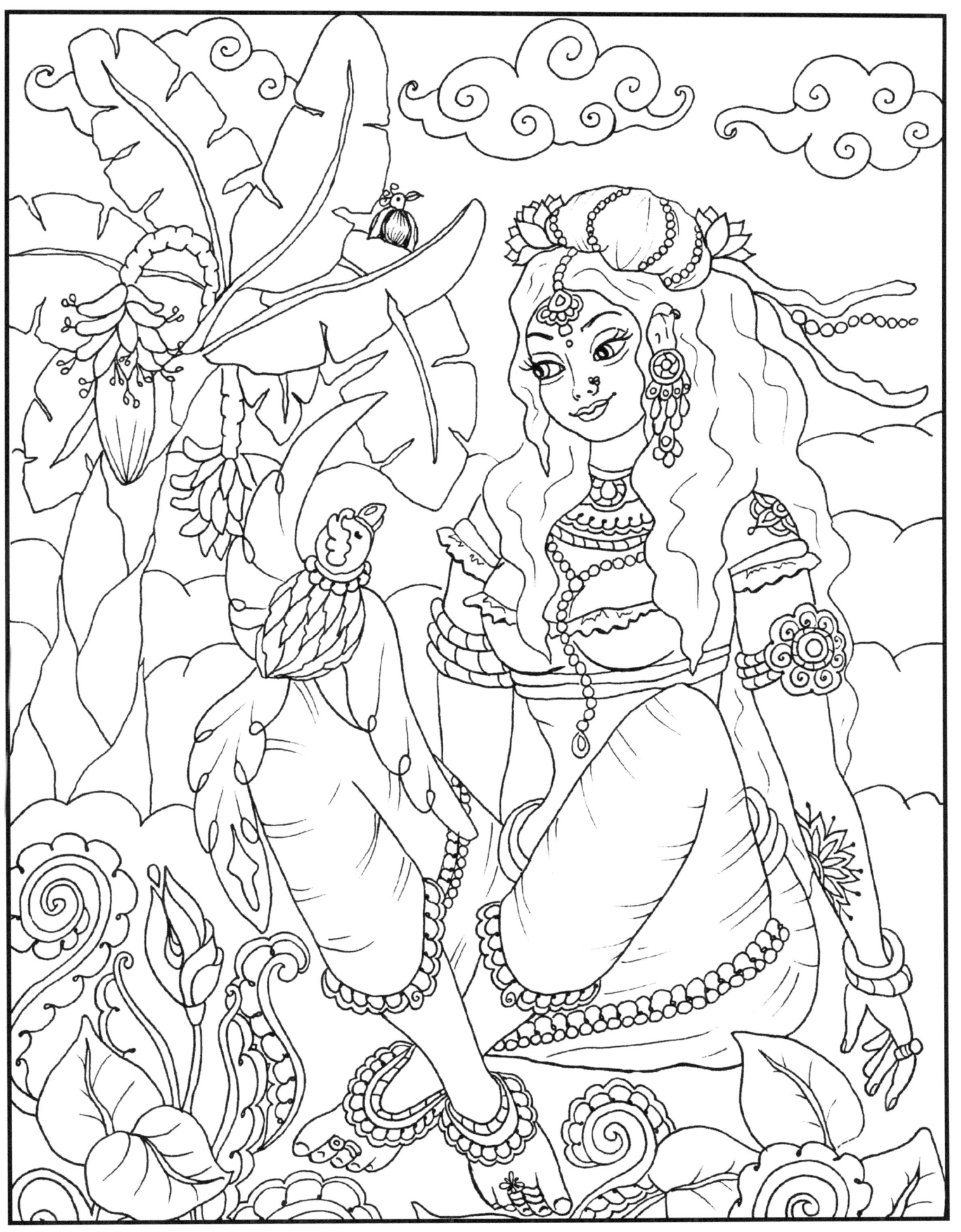

Copyright © 2021 by Katya Suresh

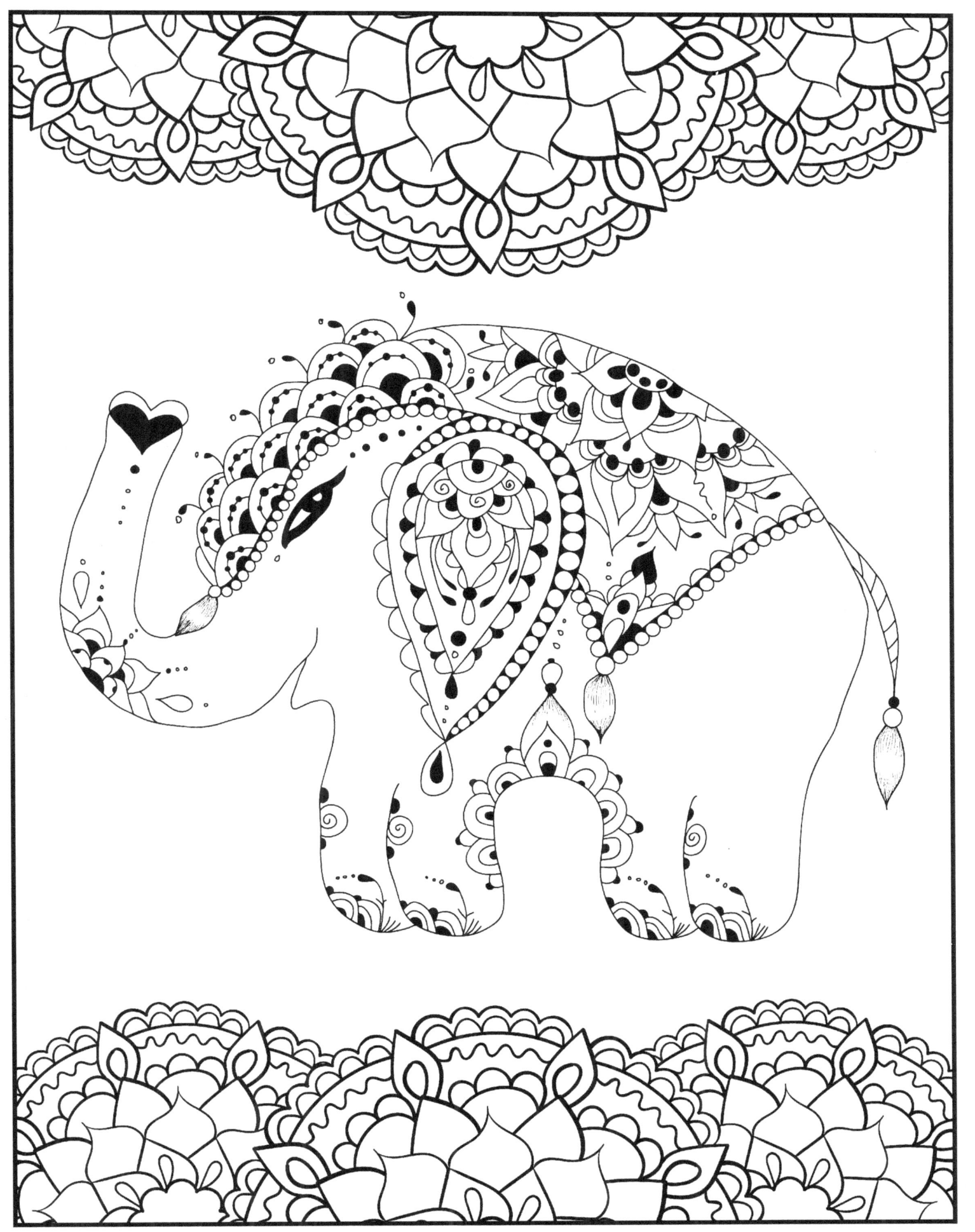

Copyright © 2021 by Katya Suresh

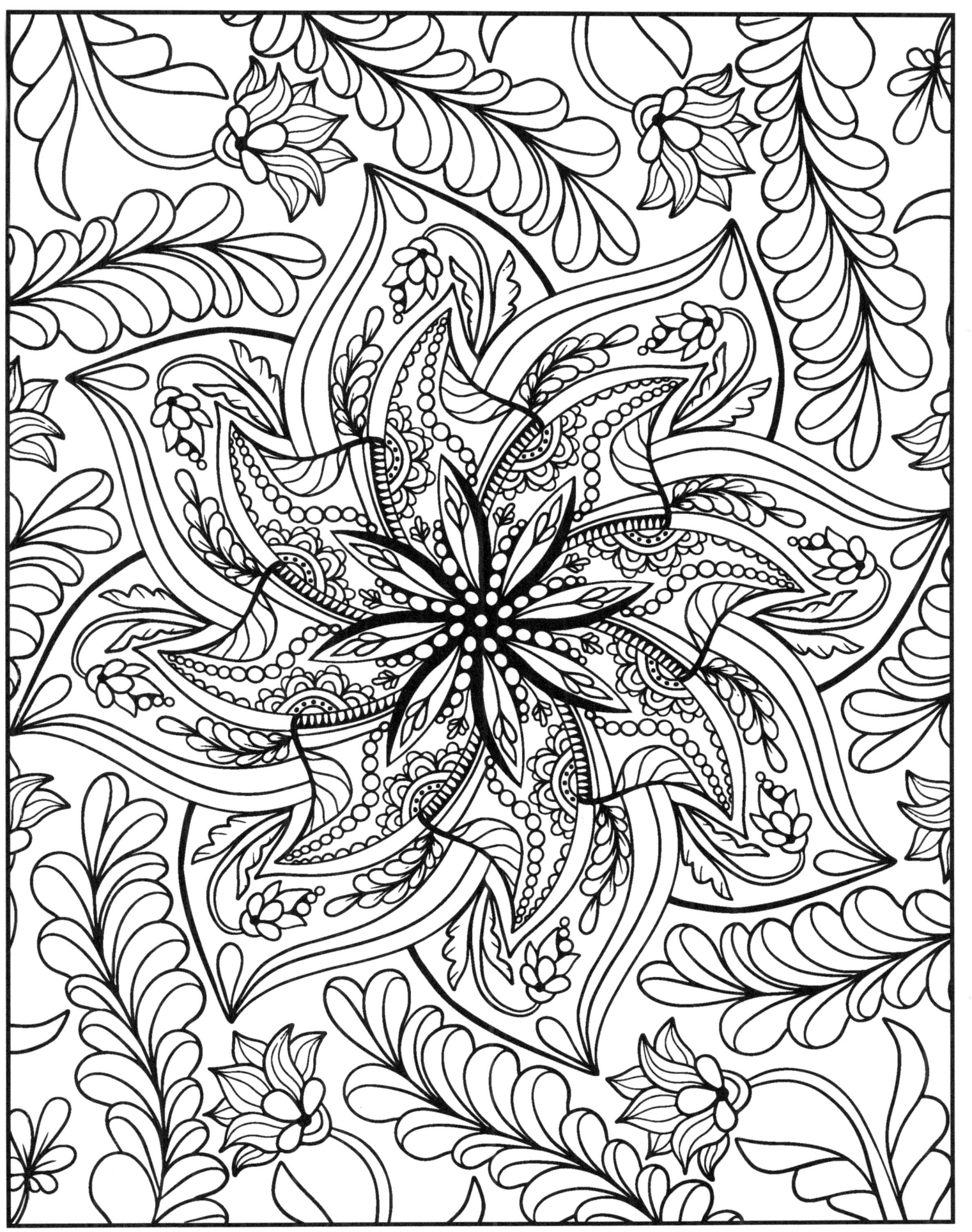

All the illustrations in this book are created by Katya Suresh.

Any part of this book cannot be reproduced without written permission of the author.

@katyasuresh
https://www.behance.net/katyasuresh
katyasureshart@gmail.com

www.ingramcontent.com/pod-product-compliance
Lightning Source LLC
Chambersburg PA
CBHW080622220526
45466CB00010B/3435